Using Context Clues To Help Kids Tackle ✳ Unfamiliar Words ✳

by Helen Zeitzoff

New York ❀ Toronto ❀ London ❀ Auckland ❀ Sydney
Mexico City ❀ New Delhi ❀ Hong Kong ❀ Buenos Aires

Teaching Resources

Cover and interior design by Kelli Thompson
Interior illustration by Margeaux Lucas
ISBN: 0-439-52477-6

3 4 5 6 7 8 9 10   40   11 10 09 08 07 06

Contents

Tools for Reading

Good readers derive meaning from many types of cues, or signals, in the texts they read. As they misread or encounter unfamiliar words, they may use three types of cues to help them identify the correct word and read on. **Graphophonic** cues, or letter combinations and their corresponding sounds, tell the reader how to pronounce the word. For example, a good reader can use the final consonants to distinguish *took* from *tool*. **Syntactic** cues, or the grammatical function of words, highlight the role of words in a sentence. For example, in the sentence *Let's record our song and play it back*, an accurate pronunciation of the word *record* is re*CORD (rather than RE*cord), because it functions as a verb, signaling the action, rather than as a noun. Finally, **semantic** cues, or the ideas provided by other words, reveal the meanings of unfamiliar words. In the sentence *Billy abhors taking that awful-tasting medicine*, a reader can infer that *abhors* means *dislikes*, since the medicine he must take is described as "awful-tasting."

When readers effectively find and use these cues in concert, they read with greater fluency and comprehension. In classrooms, we call making meaning from a variety of cues in the text **using context clues**.

About This Book

This book places student readers in the role of word detectives. It provides eight effective strategies for using context clues. Like good sleuths, students apply the strategies they learn to solve the meanings of unfamiliar words. Each unit offers instruction ideas, skills practice, and plenty of helpful tips that guide students to use each skill independently—and gain confidence as resourceful readers.

In this book you'll find:
✓ eight strategies for using context clues effectively
✓ mini-lessons and instruction ideas to make the strategies stick
✓ student reference pages that explain each strategy and give examples of how to use it
✓ reproducible pages that give students practice with each strategy
✓ student strategy sheets that summarize each section

How to Use This Book

This book is divided into four units, starting with the most basic "first aid" context-clue strategies (primarily semantic cues) and moving to more specific strategies in the second through fourth chapters (graphophonic, syntactic, and semantic cues). You may want to begin with the basics in Unit 1 and work through the eight strategies sequentially or focus on one target area at a time. Whatever order you choose, be sure to read the instruction ideas on the teacher page that opens the unit and teach students the strategies outlined on the student reference page. Students may complete the activity pages independently, in pairs, or in small groups. An answer key is included on pages 79–81.

The Eight Context Clues Strategies

First-Aid Strategies:
(Unit 1)

Strategy 1 Find nearby key words for clues about the meaning of a word.

Strategy 2 Use story titles or reading topics to predict words you'll read.

Strategy 3 Look at pictures as you read for clues about unfamiliar words.

Graphophonic Cues
& Strategies (Letter-Sound):
(Unit 2)

Strategy 4 Use letter-sound clues to read words correctly.

a. Use beginning letters, vowels, and ending letters to sound out unfamiliar words.

b. Look at vowel patterns and try out sounds they can make.

c. Separate the word into syllables.

Syntactic Cues
& Strategies (Grammar):
(Unit 3)

Strategy 5 Use grammar clues to identify an unfamiliar word.

a. Identify nouns by locating noun determiners.

b. Identify verbs as action words that follow the subject noun.

c. Identify adjectives as words that describe nouns.

d. Identify adverbs as words that describe verbs.

Strategy 6 Use key words in a passage to find a word's meaning.

a. Use keys words to find synonyms.

b. Use key words to find a synonym in the passage.

c. Use key words to check words with multiple meanings.

d. Use key words to find the meanings of unfamiliar phrases (idiomatic expressions).

Semantic Cues
& Strategies (Meaning):
(Unit 4)

Strategy 7 Use signal words to find synonyms and antonyms for an unfamiliar word.

a. Look for these words to signal synonyms: *or, is, is called, is known as, are, are called, are known as, was, was called, was known as, means, tells,* and *such as.*

b. Look for the word *but* to signal antonyms or opposite meanings.

Strategy 8 Use pictures to think of synonyms for an unfamiliar word.

Use the Clues! For the Teacher

This unit introduces students to context clues and helps them practice three essential "first aid" strategies for finding the meanings of unfamiliar words in the context of the sentences they read.

Strategy 1 Find nearby key words for clues about the meaning of a word.

Activities for Strategy 1:

* Use circled words in sentences as clues to choose an appropriate substitute for a missing word.
* Use clues in sentences to determine if the correct word is used in context.
* Circle words in sentences that provide clues to a missing or unknown word.

Strategy 2 Use story titles or reading topics to predict words you'll read.

Activities for Strategy 2:

* Use story titles to predict possible words that may appear in a reading selection.
* Eliminate words that do not relate to the context.

Strategy 3 Look at pictures as you read for clues about unfamiliar words.

Activity for Strategy 3:

* Use pictures and other graphics to find hints about the meaning of unfamiliar words.

INTRODUCTORY MINI-LESSON

Detective work has to do with clues. Set up four "mystery" boxes, each with one of the following: mittens, pencil, toothbrush, key. Show students a picture of a detective and discuss what good detectives do: they look for clues and put the clues together to solve a mystery. Tell students that they are going to practice being word detectives so they will be able to figure out on their own the words they don't know when they're reading. Introduce them to word detective work by reading aloud the sentence clues provided and inviting them to name the object in each box. Ask students to share the key word clues they used to solve the mystery. Explain that they have just used context clues to figure out the meanings of missing words.

Sample sentences with clue words circled:

Box 1: My (woolen) _____ keep my (hands warm). Sometimes these _____ (get wet) when I make a snowball.

Box 2: Ben (sharpens) his _____ before he starts (writing).

Box 3. My (teeth) look so (bright) and (clean) when I use my _____ (after each meal).

Box 4: Sally can't find the (shiny) _____ to (unlock) her (front door).

STRATEGY AND PRACTICE PAGES

Distribute copies of page 7 to students. Read aloud and discuss the definitions and the examples to be sure students understand how to use these strategies before they begin.

Note: Pages 15–17 require you to check students' articulation of the unfamiliar words. You may want to do this exercise in small groups or to meet individually with students.

TIPS FOR TEACHING FIRST-AID STRATEGIES

1. Model how to use the three strategies described on this page and on page 7. Explain your problem-solving process using a sentence or passage from your read-aloud literature or a favorite book.
2. Provide plenty of real-world examples of unfamiliar words in the context of a sentence or passage from newspaper articles, advertisements, and social studies or science textbooks.
3. Encourage students to evaluate the titles of stories they read and make predictions about vocabulary words they might find in the story. This will help them anticipate words that may be difficult to sound out.
4. Display pictures from magazines, newspapers, and cartoons for students. Have them complete sentences using picture clues for missing words.
5. Let students practice highlighting clue words to provide support for their answers.

Use the Clues! For Students

Psst! Reading detectives find **context clues**.

What are *context clues*? Context clues are hints from other words, pictures, and story titles in your reading that help you find a missing word or read unfamiliar words.

How to Use Context Clues

Strategy 1: Find nearby key words for clues about the meaning of a word.

> **Example:** Mother put the (cookies) in the _____ to (bake) for twenty-five minutes.

> **Answer:** *oven.* Cookies are placed in an oven to bake.

Strategy 2: Use story titles or reading topics to predict words you'll read.

> **Example:** Title: **Spaceship in My Backyard**
> The strange creatures were _____ from a far away planet.

> **Answer:** *aliens.* The title "Spaceship in My Backyard" sounds like a science-fiction story. You may predict that the story will be about *aliens, creatures, antennae,* and so on.

Strategy 3: Look at pictures as you read for clues about unfamiliar words.

> **Example:**

> Jane looks at the _____ to read a message.

> **Answer:** *monitor.* The screen you look at to read your messages is called a *monitor.*

Get Ready for Detective Work!

In this unit you will:

* use key words in a sentence to determine a missing word.
* predict vocabulary words using story titles or subject material.
* use picture clues to read words.

Find nearby key words for clues about the meaning of a word.

Name_____ Date_____

Reading Detective Practice #1

Directions: Read the sentence and skip the missing word.
Look for key words circled **before** and **after** the missing word.
Reread the sentence with the word you chose to make sure it fits.

> **Example:**
> Bob (used) his new _____ to (take pictures) of the beautiful mountains.
>   paint   camera   hike
>
> **Answer:** *camera.* Bob would use a camera to take pictures of the mountains.

1. (Thunder) boomed and _____ (flashed) in the (sky) during the (storm).
   girls   paintings   lightning

2. The _____ (rushed) to get the (injured) boy (to the hospital).
        horses   ambulance   circus

3. Pat got a _____ from the (toolbox) and (banged the nail) into the wood.
        soap   pen   hammer

4. Thomas is (at home) and (sick) with a (bad) _____ and a (cough).
        aspirin   cold   medicine

5. Lee (feels) _____ about (telling his mom he broke the computer).
        excited   joyous   worried

6. "Get the _____ and (clear the snow) from the sidewalk," said Dad.
        shovels   boots   dustpans

Find nearby key words for clues about the meaning of a word.

Name_____ Date_____

Reading Detective Practice #2

Directions: Read the sentence and skip the missing word.
Look for key words circled **before** and **after** the missing word.
Reread the sentence with the word you chose to make sure it fits.

All Kinds of Food

turkey

popcorn

ice cube

tomato

spaghetti

hot dog

ice cream

apples

1. Tom (snacks) on (crunchy), (buttery) _____ at the (movies).

2. Mother uses (tasty) (red) and (green) _____ in her (fruit pies).

3. (Chocolate) or (vanilla) _____ is the best (cold treat) in the summer.

4. I like (mustard) and (relish) on my _____ .

5. The school cafeteria serves _____ (with) (gravy, peas, potatoes, and) (pumpkin pie) for (Thanksgiving lunch).

6. My three-year-old brother has (sauce) on his face and (meat) on his bib as he picks up a (string) of _____ from the (bowl).

7. Place another _____ in the glass to (keep the drink) nice and (cool).

8. Richard (cut) some (carrots), a _____, and a (cucumber) for the (salad).

Using Context Clues To Help Kids Tackle Unfamiliar Words   **9**

Find nearby key words for clues about the meaning of a word.

Name_____ Date_____

Reading Detective Practice #3

Directions: Read the sentence and skip the missing word.
Look for key words circled **before** and **after** the missing word.
Reread the sentence with the word you chose to make sure it fits.

sundae	jelly	cake	beans
cob	pancakes	sugar	cereal

1. Tanya loves to eat (peanut butter) and _____ (sandwiches) for lunch.

2. Dad uses _____ to (sweeten) his (coffee).

3. Bill loves to eat (corn on the) _____ for (dinner).

4. I (pour) lots of (maple syrup) on my _____.

5. Marvin's (Ice Cream Parlor) makes the best (hot fudge) _____.

6. Every morning I have a (bowl) of _____ for (breakfast).

7. (String) _____ are my favorite (vegetable).

8. Mother (bakes) a (chocolate) _____ for Nan's (birthday).

Find nearby key words for clues about the meaning of a word.

Name_____ Date_____

Reading Detective Practice #4

Directions: Fill in each blank with the farm word that makes sense.
Circle the nearby key words that helped you.

On the Farm

house

barn

cows

horse

tractor

hay

1. Farmer Brown rides on a _____ to clear the land.

2. Early in the morning, the farmer leaves his _____. After a long day's work, he returns to be with his family.

3. The farmer's _____ provide his family with milk.

4. Farmer Brown puts _____ in the horse's stall.

5. When the _____ does a good job, the farmer gives it a piece of sugar.

6. The farmer has a big red _____ where he stores tools and keeps horses.

—————— **Can You Name the Animals on Your Own?** ——————

Directions: Fill in each blank with the name of the animal that completes each
sentence. Circle the nearby key words that helped you.

1. Every morning on the farm, the _____ crows, "Cock a doodle doo."

2. The _____ like to play in the mud, eat, and snort, "Oink, oink."

3. The farmer shaves the _____. The wool is used to make warm clothes.

4. In November the farmer picks a big _____ for Thanksgiving dinner.

Use story titles or reading topics to predict words you'll read.

Name_____ Date_____

Reading Detective Practice #5

Directions: Read each title and circle the words you would expect to find in the story

> **Example:** Story title: "The Fourth of July"
>
> (fireworks)   (celebrate)   snow   (picnic)   winter   (holiday)
>
> **Answer:** The story "The Fourth of July" might include words like *fireworks*, *celebrate*, *picnic*, and *holiday*.

1. The Baseball Champ

hitter   fielder   football   coach   strike   puck   umpire

2. A Little Garden

flowers   hose   shovel   pencil   vegetables   fish   traffic

3. My Dog Felix

obeys   barks   bowl   fishing pole   bone   chirps

4. The Haunted House

strange   old   beautiful   scary   peaceful   bats   creaks

5. A Swimming Race

field goal   diving   swing   shallow   theater   goggles   flippers

6. Summer Camp

bunk   hikes   homework   counselors   activities   book report

Using Context Clues To Help Kids Tackle Unfamiliar Words

Use story titles or reading topics to predict words you'll read.

Name_____ Date_____

Reading Detective Practice #6

Directions: Read each title or subject and cross out the word that most likely would not be found in the story or passage.

1. Subject: **cats**

   purr   whiskers   rowboat   tabby   fur   flying

2. Subject: **circus**

   tiger   watermelon   trapeze   ringmaster   clowns   elephants

3. Subject: **city**

   sidewalks   crowd   taxicabs   skyscraper   mountain climbing   traffic

4. Title: **The Missing Money**

   detective   searching   clues   jungle   mystery   thief

5. Title: **The Secret Cave**

   explore   dark   hidden   piano lessons   dangerous

6. Subject: **geography**

   mountains   rivers   oceans   multiply   lakes   islands

Use story titles or reading topics to predict words you'll read.

Name_____ Date_____

Reading Detective Practice #7

Directions: Read the title of the story below.
Circle the vocabulary words you might find in the passage.
Then read the story and use context clues to write the word that makes sense on the line.

Kate's Birthday

| cake | games | recess | prizes | spelling | presents | friends | jungle |

Yesterday was Kate's birthday party. Six _____ came to Kate's house.

Kate and her friends ate pizza for lunch. They enjoyed _____ and

ice cream for dessert. After lunch, Kate opened _____ and the

children played party _____. Next, a magician entertained the kids

with his tricks. Then, Kate handed colorful party bags to her friends. The bags

were filled with card tricks, _____, and lollipops. As Kate waved

good-bye to her friends, she said to her mom, "Today was a wonderful day."

Directions: Predict other words you might find in a story titled "Kate's Birthday."

_____   _____   _____   _____

Strategy 3

Look at pictures as you read for clues about unfamiliar words.

Name_____ Date_____

Reading Detective Practice #8

Directions: Read these sentences to your teacher.
Use the pictures for clues to reading each word in **bold**.

Example:

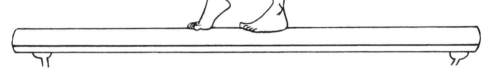

Kim walks slowly across the **balance** beam. How do you say this word?

Answer: BAH*lens. Kim is doing gymnastics. She is walking on a balance beam.

⋯⋯⋯ **At the Store** ⋯⋯⋯

	Teacher Notes:

1. Amani pays the clerk at the cash **register** for her new shoes.

register

2. Amani hands the clerk a **coupon** to buy the shoes on sale.

coupon

3. The clerk hands Amani a **receipt** after she has paid for the shoes.

receipt

Using Context Clues To Help Kids Tackle Unfamiliar Words   🐾 🐾 🐾 🐾 🐾 🐾 🐾 🐾 **15**

Reading Detective Practice #8 (continued)

| | Teacher Notes: |

4. Amani takes the **escalator** up to the next floor.

escalator

5. Amani visits the **jewelry** department to buy a bracelet for her friend.

jewelry

6. Amani takes the **elevator** down to the first floor.

elevator

7. Amani buys **perfume** as a gift for her mom.

perfume

8. Amani leaves the store with many **bundles** in her arms.

bundles

Strategy 3

Look at pictures as you read for clues about unfamiliar words.

Name_____ Date_____

Reading Detective Practice #9

Directions: Use picture clues to identify the missing words in the sentences.
Fill in the missing words and read the sentences to your teacher.

The Doctor's Office

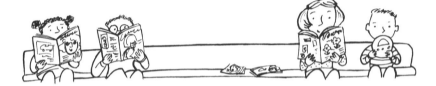

1. The _____ are waiting to see the doctor.

_____

2. The _____ takes information from Mom.

_____

3. The doctor checks my heartbeat with a _____.

_____

4. Doctor Howard writes a _____ for medicine.

Word Clues
doctor
prescription
nurse
story
check-up
patients
stethoscope

Name_____ Date_____

Reading Detective Practice #10

Directions: Use picture clues to identify the missing word in the sentence. Fill in the missing word and reread the sentence to see if it makes sense.

The King's Castle

Word Clues
plate
crown
king
throne
servant
balcony
princess
castle

1. The king sits on his _____. Soon he will meet with his subjects.

2. The _____ brings food to the king.

3. The king wears a _____ on his head.

4. The king knows that his subjects are waiting for him to give a speech. The king stands on the _____ waving to the crowd below.

5. The king's daughter, the _____, wears a long dress and stands beside him.

Tracks to Follow!

First-Aid Strategies

Strategy 1

Find nearby key words for clues about the meaning of a word.

Example: The _____ galloped away from the barn.

*Ask yourself,
What gallops?
What lives in a barn?*

Answer: *horse.*

Strategy 2

Use story titles or reading topics to predict the words you'll read.

Example: Story title: "Summer Camp"

The story could include the words *hiking, swimming, campsite, campfire, counselors,* and so on.

The camp _____ led the children to the trail.

Answer: *counselors.*

Strategy 3

Look at pictures as you read for clues about unfamiliar words.

Example:

The _____ is working on the car right now.

Answer: *mechanic.*

Use the Clues! For the Teacher

This unit helps students use their knowledge of letters and corresponding sounds (graphophonic elements) in tandem with the contextual strategies from Chapter 1 to discriminate among word choices, read unfamiliar words, and prevent or correct miscues (incorrect reading of known words). Note: Before you begin this unit, be sure that students have a solid phonics foundation. They will be asked to recognize consonants and vowel blends and break words into syllables.

In this unit students will use the following strategy to decode unfamiliar words.

Strategy 4 Use letter-sound clues to read words correctly.

a. Use beginning letters, vowels, and ending letters to sound out unfamiliar words.
b. Look at vowel patterns and try out different sounds they can make.
c. Separate the word into syllables.

Activities for Strategy 4:

❀ Practice recognizing the phonemic differences in words.

❀ Use beginning letters to help determine words in context.

❀ Use highlighted key words to help select missing words in sentences.

❀ Check for accuracy using both contextual and graphophonic cues.

INTRODUCTORY MINI-LESSON

When students read, they often use the beginning letters of a word to sound it out. Beginning readers may stop there and call out any word with the same initial sound as the word they are looking at, whether it makes sense or not. Good readers employ self-checking strategies. They make sure that the word they read makes sense in the context of the sentence and that they've read the word correctly by carefully matching the sounds to the letters in the rest of the word. To encourage students to use graphophonic cues along with context clues, write the sample sentences in set 1 on the chalkboard. Review the examples, asking students to show the letter-sound differences among the answer choices and explain the meanings of the words as used in the sentences.

Sample sentences (set 1):

1. We had fried ch_____ for dinner.
   chairs   chicken   chipmunks
2. What is the pr_____ of the new car?
   practice   preach   price

Make sure students are aware that they must focus on the letters to sound out a word correctly. Write the sentences from the sample sentences in set 2 on the chalkboard and read them with the incorrect word. Discuss with students why the word is incorrect and what the letter-sound clues tell them to say.

Sample sentences (set 2):

1. Jeff found a shiny 5-cent **cone** on the sidewalk.
   coin
2. Mr. Frank **close** the shiny green car.
   chose
3. Did the boys **prance** for the game?
   practice

STRATEGY AND PRACTICE PAGES:

Distribute copies of page 21 to students. Read aloud and discuss the letter-sound clues and examples to be sure students understand how to use this strategy. The practice pages begin with more support, listing strategies and examples, and gradually provide less help as students gain confidence using the strategy.

Note: Page 22 requires you to check students' articulation of the unfamiliar words. You may want to have students read additional practice pages aloud to you to assess the application of this skill.

TIPS FOR TEACHING GRAPHOPHONIC CUES STRATEGIES:

1. Model the use of letter-sound clues for reading unfamiliar words in context during lessons in all subject areas.
2. Challenge students to use the letter-sound clues to decode unfamiliar words from selected reading passages (novels, newspapers, magazines, science and social studies texts, and so on).
3. Remind students that using letter-sound clues and double-checking that the word they've chosen makes sense can help them become stronger readers.

Use the Clues! For Students

Psst! Reading detectives can figure out how to read words by using **letter-sound clues.**

What are *letter-sound clues*? These are the sounds that match the letters of the alphabet and their combinations. Good readers sound out words by making the right sounds for the letters in the words.

How to Use Letter-Sound Clues

Strategy 4: Use letter-sound clues to read words correctly.

a. Use beginning letters, vowels, and ending letters to sound out unfamiliar words.

> **Example:** The **referee** (blew the whistle) because the (player went out of bounds).

> **Answer: re*fer*EE**
> * The beginning letter *r* goes with someone who blows a whistle in a game.
> * *Referee* has three vowels sounds: short *e*, *er*, long *e*.
> * A *referee* is the person who blows the whistle when a player is out of bounds.

b. Look at vowel patterns and try out different sounds they can make.

> **Example:** It is good to take a **break** and **read** a good book.

> **Answer:** *ea* has the long *a* sound in *break* and the long *e* sound in *read*.

c. Separate the word into syllables.

> **Example:** You are learning the **fundamentals** of context clues.

> **Answer:** There are four syllables—*fun   da   men   tals.*

Get Ready for Detective Work!

In this unit you will sound out words by:

* using beginning letters, vowels, and ending letters.
* looking at vowel patterns and trying out sounds for letter combinations.
* breaking the words into syllables.

Strategy 4a. Use beginning letters, vowels, and ending letters to sound out unfamiliar words.

Strategy 4b. Look at vowel patterns and try out sounds for letter combinations.

Strategy 4c. Separate the word into syllables.

Use letter-sound clues to read words correctly.

Name_____ Date_____

Reading Detective Practice #11

Directions: Read these sentences to your teacher.
Use context clues and letter-sound clues to correctly read the words in **bold**.

Example:

The (air) **conditioning** is turned on to (cool the house) on (hot summer days).

Clues:

- "air," "cool the house," "hot summer days"
- The beginning letters tell us to say "con."
- A vowel sound is needed for *i*, the letters *tion* make the "shun" sound, and the ending suffix is *-ing*

Answer: conditioning (con*DI*shun*ing).

---

1. Many years had passed and Jim did not **recognize** his old friend.

2. That big, shiny car is very **expensive**.

3. We **celebrate** the holiday with a big family dinner.

4. Mrs. Smiley told the students to use their **imaginations** and write about living in space.

5. Jack was in a difficult **situation** and needed help.

6. The doctor wants Bill to take this **medication** for his allergies.

7. Jason was very **thirsty** at the end of the race.

8. The game is **canceled** if it rains.

9. Mr. Biggins **demonstrates** the correct way to test **chemicals** in the science experiment.

Strategy 4

Strategy 4a. Use beginning letters, vowels, and ending letters to sound out unfamiliar words.
Strategy 4b. Look at vowel patterns and try out sounds for letter combinations.
Strategy 4c. Separate the word into syllables.

Use letter-sound clues to read words correctly.

Name_____ Date_____

Reading Detective Practice #12

Directions: Follow Strategy 4 to be sure the word you choose is correct.

1. The school band is getting ready to march in the holiday p_____.

   party   parade

2. Felix gets plenty of ex_____ at the gym.

   exercise   excitement

3. Last week our class had a s_____ because the teacher was sick.

   submarine   substitute

4. Dad parked the car in the g_____ so it did not get covered with snow.

   garbage   garage

5. Paul is too big to fit into his brother's l_____ wagon.

   listen   little

6. The wonderful sm_____ is coming from the cake baking in the oven.

   smell   smoke

7. The kids like to r_____ the leaves in the yard.

   rattle   rake

8. A dentist tells the boys and girls to use a t_____ after each meal.

   toenail   toothbrush

9. Our team tied the s_____ at half time.

   score   scare

Strategy 4

Strategy 4a. Use beginning letters, vowels, and ending letters to sound out unfamiliar words.

Strategy 4b. Look at vowel patterns and try out sounds for letter combinations.

Strategy 4c. Separate the word into syllables.

Use letter-sound clues to read words correctly.

Name_____ Date_____

Reading Detective Practice #13

Directions: Follow Strategy 4 to be sure the word you choose is correct.

1. The men were ready to climb the highest _____ in the world.

                                  mouse   mountain   moose

2. There was _____ on Mike's hand from the cut.

       brook   blood   broom

3. The pirate ship was searching for the sunken _____.

                             treasure   treaty   trapeze

4. The campers went _____ riding on the new trail.

        horseback   houseboat   horseshoe

5. The _____ boy returned the lost money to the owner.

    hairy   horrible   honest

6. Mr. and Mrs. Cooper went to the _____ store to buy a new sofa and chair for the living room.

                    furniture   furnace   future

7. The weather _____ predicts snow for tomorrow.

       forward   forecast   forest

8. Use _____ when crossing a busy street.

   cattle   coast   caution

Strategy 4a. Use beginning letters, vowels, and ending letters to sound out unfamiliar words.
Strategy 4b. Look at vowel patterns and try out sounds for letter combinations.
Strategy 4c. Separate the word into syllables.

Use letter-sound clues to read words correctly.

Name_____ Date_____

Reading Detective Practice #14

Directions: Use Strategy 4 to see if the word in **bold** is correct.
Circle *Yes* or *No* to show your answer.
If the word is incorrect, write the correct word on the line provided.

	Is the word correct?		Write the correct word.

1. The school nurse put a **banana** on my cut. Yes No _____

2. City streets have lots of **traffic**. Yes No _____

3. **Multiply** 7 and 5 and the answer is 35. Yes No _____

4. The **hospital** flew over the highway to report on the accident. Yes No _____

5. Raven said, "I am **flat** from eating so much." Yes No _____

6. Carlos won first place for running the **funniest**. Yes No _____

7. You can **wash** the movie on television. Yes No _____

8. Some birds **flip** south in winter. Yes No _____

9. The **president** is the leader of our country. Yes No _____

Name_____ Date_____

Reading Detective Practice #15

Directions: Read the story below and fill in the blanks with the correct word.
Use the meaning of the story to help you figure out the missing words.
Use letter-sound clues to check that you are reading the word correctly.

A Helping Hand

Jeff and Brianna were raking leaves in their yard. All of a _____ they
seven, sudden

_____ a loud crash. They ran out to the sidewalk and saw there
heard, hurried

had been a car _____ at the _____ of Main Street and
accent, accident **interest, intersection**

Rogers Road. The drivers of both cars were talking. Kids sat inside both cars, but

no one had been hurt. Jeff and Brianna _____ to play games with the
offered, opened

children in the yard while their parents discussed the accident. Both drivers were

_____ to Jeff and Brianna for their _____ and for taking
great, grateful **concern, curiosity**

care of the children. Jeff and Brianna were glad to have helped the drivers

and the kids. Later that day, their parents _____ Jeff and Brianna for
practiced, praised

the kindness they showed to others.

Tracks to Follow!

Letter-Sound Clues

Strategy 4

Use letter-sound clues to read words correctly.

a. **Check beginning letters, vowels, and ending letters.**

   Example: We have indoor recess today! The rain will **continue** (all day long).

What word starts with "con" and means "to go on" or "to keep happening"?

   Answer: con*TIN*yew

b. **Try out other sounds for letter combinations.**

   Example: The **chemist** received an award for making a new medicine.

   Answer: *Ch* can make the *ch*, *k*, and *sh* sounds. In *chemist*, the *ch* makes a *k* sound, as in the word *chemical*. A *chemist* works with chemicals to make medicines and other things.

c. **Separate the word into syllables.**

   Example: The girls can **harmonize** when they sing together.

   Answer: There are three syllables—*har   mo   nize*.

🔍 Use the Clues! For the Teacher

In this unit, students use their grammar skills and the syntax of the sentence to make a good guess at an unknown or missing word. Supported by the first-aid and letter-sound strategies in Units 1 and 2, students learn to determine the meaning of unknown words by identifying the roles they play. Note: Before you begin this unit, be sure that students understand the basic parts of speech, especially nouns and verbs, which are featured on practice pages 30–38. Older students can be challenged to identify adjectives and adverbs, featured on practice pages 39–49.

Strategy 5 Use grammar clues to identify an unfamiliar word.
a. Identify nouns by locating noun determiners (*a*, *an*, *the*).
b. Identify verbs as action words that follow the subject noun. Verbs often take these forms: (1) root and (2) root + the ending *-s*, *-ing*, or *-ed*.
c. Identify adjectives as words that describe nouns. Adjectives tell *what kind*, *how many*, *whose*, or *which*.
d. Identify adverbs as words that describe verbs. Adverbs tell *how*, *when*, or *where*.

Activities for Strategy 5:
❀ Use noun determiners to locate nouns in sentences.
❀ Use subject nouns to locate verbs in sentences.
❀ Use nouns to locate adjectives in sentences.
❀ Use verbs to locate adverbs in sentences.
❀ Select the noun, verb, adjective, or adverb that fits the context of a sentence.

INTRODUCTORY MINI-LESSON

Tell students that grammar clues help readers figure out the jobs that unknown words are doing in sentences. To review the parts of speech they'll need to know in the activities, show them the Branches of a Sentence model. Draw a simple tree with four branches labeled *Nouns*, *Verbs*, *Adjectives*, and *Adverbs*. Write the sample sentences provided on sentence strips and have student volunteers place them on the branches that identify the part of speech underlined on the strip. Make sure students can explain the job of each word in the sentence.

Sample sentences
1. Jacob <u>raced</u> around the track.
   (*Raced*, a verb, shows the action that Jacob did. Clue: *-ed* ending.)
2. Can you sleep on a <u>firm</u> mattress?
   (*Firm* is an adjective that describes the kind of *mattress*. Clue: describes *mattress*, a noun.)
3. The cups are on the <u>table</u>.
   (*Cups* and *table* are nouns. They name things. Clue: The noun determiner *the* signals a noun.)
4. Pat ran <u>quickly</u> to get out of the rain.
   (*Quickly* is an adverb. It tells how Pat ran. Clue: describes *ran*, a verb.)

STRATEGY AND PRACTICE PAGES

Distribute copies of page 29 to students. Read aloud and discuss grammar clues and the examples to be sure students understand how to use this strategy.

TIPS FOR TEACHING SYNTACTIC-CUE STRATEGIES:

1. For extra practice with parts of speech, play a game similar to *Jeopardy!* with these categories: *Nouns*, *Verbs*, *Adjectives*, *Adverbs*, *All Parts of Speech*. In each square, write a sentence with a missing vocabulary word. To answer, students must supply an appropriate word. The last category is the most difficult: Students must identify the missing part of speech before supplying an appropriate word.

2. Make copies of reading selections from newspapers, science and social studies textbooks, travel brochures, and other nonfiction materials. Underline or highlight difficult vocabulary words, and ask students to name what parts of speech they are. Or blank out the difficult words and have students identify which parts of speech are missing. Ask them to suggest words that fit in the blanks.

Use the Clues! For Students

Psst! Reading detectives figure out the job each word does in a sentence by using **grammar clues**.

What are *grammar clues*?
They tell whether an unknown word is a noun, verb, adjective, or adverb.

Strategy 5: Use grammar clues to identify an unfamiliar word.

a. Identify nouns by locating noun determiners. (*a, an, the, this, that, your, my, their, his, her, many, some,* and so on)

> **Example: Many** strangers came to **our** aid after **the** earthquake.

> **Answer:** *Strangers, aid,* and *earthquake* are the nouns in this sentence. The determiners **many, our,** and **the** signal these nouns.

b. Identify verbs as action words that follow the subject noun. Verbs often take these forms: (1) root; (2) root + the ending *-s, -ing,* or *-ed.*

> **Example:** The **teacher** explained the steps to the division problem.

> **Answer:** *Explained* is the verb in this sentence. The action word *explained* follows *teacher,* the subject noun. It tells what the teacher did and has the *-ed* ending.

c. Identify adjectives as words that describe nouns. Adjectives tell *what kind, how many, whose,* or *which.*

> **Example:** The comfortable **sofa** can seat six **people**.

> **Answer:** *Comfortable* and *six* are adjectives. *Comfortable* describes the kind of sofa, and *six* tells how many people.

d. Identify adverbs as words that describe verbs. Adverbs tell *how, when,* or *where.*

> **Example:** John **ran** quickly to catch the bus.

> **Answer:** *Quickly* describes the verb *ran.* The adverb *quickly* tells how Jon ran. The suffix *-ly* is a clue that *quickly* is an adverb.

Get Ready for Detective Work!
In this unit you will:
- use noun determiners to locate nouns in sentences.
- use subject nouns to locate verbs in sentences.
- use nouns to locate adjectives in sentences.
- use verbs to locate adverbs in sentences.

Use grammar clues to identify an unfamiliar word.

Name_____ Date_____

Reading Detective Practice #16

Tips!
Noun determiners are words such as *a, an, the, his, her, this, that, many,* and *your.* Usually you can find the noun one or two words after its determiner.

Directions: Circle the nouns in each sentence. Look for noun determiners in **bold**.

Example: An apple **a** day keeps **the** doctor away.

Answer: *Apple, day,* and *doctor* are the nouns in this sentence. The determiners are **an, a,** and **the.**

1. **The** horse galloped into **the** town.

2. **The** kids rowed **their** boat around **the** lake.

3. **The** machine only takes **these** coins.

4. **The** principal used **the** microphone to speak.

5. **A** troll stood under **the** bridge.

6. **An** alligator lives in **the** swamp.

Directions: Read the sentence and choose the best noun to fill in the blank.

7. **My** _____ Tom and Aunt Betty visit us every Christmas.

      doctor   Uncle   children

8. The ship sails across **the** _____.

      garden   country   ocean

9. Dad was in **the** _____ preparing dinner for the family.

      city   kitchen   basement

10. **The** _____ gives the meanings of words.

      dictionary   novel   map

Use grammar clues to identify an unfamiliar word.

Name_____ Date_____

Reading Detective Practice #17

Directions: In each sentence check if the underlined noun is correct.
Circle *Yes* or *No*.
If the noun is not correct, replace it with one that makes sense.

	Is the noun correct?		Write the correct noun.
1. **The** <u>straps</u> twinkle in the sky	Yes	No	st_____
2. **The** <u>elephant</u> sucks in water with its trunk.	Yes	No	e_____
3. Ben rides **the** <u>bear</u> to school.	Yes	No	b_____
4. Mr. Smith uses **a** <u>letter</u> to reach the top shelf.	Yes	No	l_____
5. **The** <u>machine</u> can make repairs to the car.	Yes	No	m_____

Directions: Are the underlined nouns correct? If not, write the correct one on the line provided.

6. **The** <u>pillow</u> sits in the cockpit of the plane.

   p_____

7. There are **many** <u>baskets</u> for the party.

     b_____

8. Mr. Jones sits on **a** <u>bend</u> in the park.

     b_____

9. **The** <u>cabin</u> was hidden in the woods.

   c_____

Use grammar clues to identify an unfamiliar word.

Name_____ Date_____

Reading Detective Practice #18

Directions: Read the title of the story below.
Circle the nouns that you might find in the story.
Place the nouns you circled in the sentences below.
Notice the noun determiners in **bold**.

Summer Vacation

camera	**beach**	**sunscreen**	**seashells**	**recess**
clothes	**diary**	**photographs**	**goggles**	**homework**

The James family is busy packing suitcases for their vacation to Hawaii. The

weather will be hot, so they are filling their suitcases with lightweight _____.

They will pack bathing suits for the days the family spends at **the** _____.

Everyone in the family has something special that needs to go into the suitcase.

Mark wants to go snorkeling, so he packs **his** _____ to see underwater.

Julie packs **her** _____ because she wants to draw and write about **the**

beautiful _____ on the beach. Mom packs plenty of _____ to

protect everyone from the strong sun. Dad places **the** _____ in the

suitcase because he will take **the** _____ of this exciting time.

Use grammar clues to identify an unfamiliar word.

Name_____ Date_____

Reading Detective Practice #19

Directions: Fill in the noun that completes each sentence.
Notice the noun determiners in **bold**.
Check that the noun you choose fits the sentence.

| police officer   astronaut   teacher   lawyer   doctor   musician |

1. "Rockets and space are my interest," said Paul. "When I grow up I want to become **an** _____."

2. Montrose said, "I want to protect people and keep them safe in the city. One day, I hope to prevent crime when I am **a** _____."

3. Burt wants to help people who get into trouble with the law. Burt wants to become **a** _____.

4. Ali said, "I want to become **a** _____ just like Mrs. Light." Ali loves to help other kids in her class with reading and spelling.

5. Robert said, "I like to play the clarinet, trombone, and piano." He will probably become **a** _____.

6. Gloria wants to care for sick people. She will become **a** _____.

Use grammar clues to identify an unfamiliar word.

Name_____ Date_____

Reading Detective Practice #20

Directions: Circle the action word (verb) that follows each subject noun in **bold**.

> **Example:** The **team** (plays) a soccer game today.
>
> **Answer:** *Plays* is the action word following the subject noun *team*.
> *Plays* is the verb; it tells what the team does.

Tips!
Verbs often take these forms: (1) root; (2) root + the ending -s, -ing, or -ed.

1. **Policemen** protected the neighborhood.

2. **Monica** held the baby for a long time.

3. **Boys and girls** skate around the neighborhood.

4. The **class** is reading a new chapter book.

Directions: Choose the verb that fits each sentence.
Use clues **before** and **after** the blank to help you choose the verb.

5. **Natalie** _____ after sitting for a long time.   (strings, stretches)

6. **Mr. Alva** _____ wood for the fireplace.   (chops, chases)

7. The **movie** _____ at four o'clock.   (stamps, starts)

8. **Frank** _____ to catch the bus.   (rushes, raps)

9. Each **boy** _____ two glasses of milk.   (drinks, drills)

Use grammar clues to identify an unfamiliar word.

Name_____ Date_____

Reading Detective Practice #21

Directions: In each sentence, check if the underlined verb is correct.
Circle *Yes* or *No*.
If the verb is not correct, replace it with one that has the same
beginning letters and makes sense.

	Is the verb correct?		**Write the correct verb.**

1. The **firemen** <u>rested</u> people
   from the building.   Yes   No   r_____

2. The **crossing guard** <u>waved</u>
   to the children.   Yes   No   w_____

3. **Mr. Gates** <u>repaired</u> the
   broken fence.   Yes   No   r_____

4. The **boys** <u>liked</u> for the lost
   diamond ring.   Yes   No   l_____

5. **John** <u>tagged</u> the next runner.   Yes   No   t_____

6. The **player** <u>dribbled</u> the ball
   down the court.   Yes   No   dr_____

7. The boys' **team** <u>juggled</u> around
   the track.   Yes   No   j_____

8. The **pitcher** <u>thought</u> a fast ball.   Yes   No   th_____

Use grammar clues to identify an unfamiliar word.

Name_____ Date_____

Reading Detective Practice #22

Directions: Write the verb that completes each sentence.
Check that the verb you choose makes sense.

A Saturday Club Meeting: Part 1

| announced | gathered | talked | agreed | raise | liked |

The **Kids Club** _____ at Tim's house every Saturday morning. Last

Saturday, the club's **president** _____ that the club would have a yard

sale. **They** would _____ money for the school library fund. **Club members**

_____ this idea. Many **boys and girls** _____ about the old toy

they could sell. **Everyone** _____ that the sale should take place in a month

A Saturday Club Meeting: Part 2

| sold | examined | pointed | contributed | came |

Neighborhood **parents** _____ with their children to the sale. The

little **ones** _____ to the toys they wanted. Before they took out their

money, the **parents** _____ the bikes, wagons, sports equipment,

and board games. Everything was in good condition. The **toys** _____

fast. By the end of the day, everything was gone. The club members raised one

hundred dollars, which **they** _____ to the library for new books.

Use grammar clues to identify an unfamiliar word.

Name_____ Date_____

Reading Detective Practice #23

Directions: Read the dialogue in the sentences below.
Choose a more exact verb to replace "said."
Check that the verb you choose fits the sentence.

Example: "Look out! There's a snake!" ___shouted___ Bob.
~~said~~

What other verbs could replace *said*?

Answer: *Yelled* or *screamed*.

---

announced   groaned   mumbled   cautioned   advised   sobbed

---

1. Tara's mouth was full of food. I couldn't understand her as she _____ ,
~~said~~

"I don't want to be late for school."

2. Bobby _____ , "I feel sick."
~~said~~

3. "The next street has a detour, so you will have to take another route to the

stadium," _____ the policeman.
~~said~~

4. Mrs. Dixon, our teacher, _____ , "The class will take a trip to the
~~said~~

science museum next month."

5. With tears in his eyes, the little boy _____ , "I fell down and
~~said~~

skinned my knee."

6. "Get a good night's rest before you take the big test," _____ the
~~said~~

math teacher.

Using Context Clues To Help Kids Tackle Unfamiliar Words   🐾 🐾 🐾 🐾 🐾 🐾 🐾 🐾 **37**

Use grammar clues to identify an unfamiliar word.

Name_____ Date_____

Reading Detective Practice #24

Directions: Circle *noun* or *verb* to show what is missing from each sentence.
Fill in the blank with a noun or verb that fits each sentence.
There is more than one right answer for each example.

1. The children _____ at the park.   noun   verb

2. Many _____ came to hear the president's speech.   noun   verb

3. The big giant _____ everyone in town.   noun   verb

4. The _____ was launched at ten o'clock.   noun   verb

5. The _____ pulled a rabbit out of the hat.   noun   verb

6. At the beach, Alex _____ a sand castle.   noun   verb

7. A squirrel _____ around the yard.   noun   verb

8. Billy _____ a hamburger and fries.   noun   verb

9. Do you like _____ on your pizza?   noun   verb

Use grammar clues to identify an unfamiliar word.

Name_____ Date_____

Reading Detective Practice #25

Directions: Circle the adjectives that describe each noun in **bold**.

> **Example:** They played an (exciting) **game** at recess.
>
> **Answer:** The adjective *exciting* describes the noun *game*; it tells *what kind* of game took place.

1. The soft, furry **kitten** sat on my lap.

2. An old, broken-down **car** sat in the parking lot.

3. Pete found a shiny **penny**.

4. Mom told Trevor to wash his sticky **hands**.

5. Bill said, "I have a stuffy **nose**."

6. A strange, shadowy **figure** appeared at the window.

Directions: Circle all the adjectives that could describe each noun in **bold**.

7. I like to eat _____ **food**.

   salty   excited   spicy   sour   past   clever   juicy

8. A _____ **truck** drove down the street.

   dirty   squeaky   honest   noisy   angry   speedy   shiny

9. The _____ **bag** will hold the toys.

   plastic   early   striped   tasty   enormous   shivering   blue

Use grammar clues to identify an unfamiliar word.

Name_____ Date_____

Reading Detective Practice #26

Directions: Choose an adjective to describe each noun in **bold** in the sentences below.
Check that the word you choose makes sense.

> curious   rude   confused   modern   suspicious   shallow   smiling   rotten

1. Detectives followed the _____ **man** in the gray suit.

2. A _____ **boy** showed his parents the A on his math test.

3. The _____ **student** searched through science books for information.

4. Water comes up to my waist in the _____ **part** of the pool.

5. A _____ **building** has now replaced the old one.

6. The _____ **person** pushed ahead of everyone in the ticket line.

7. You wouldn't want to eat this _____ **apple**.

8. The _____ **campers** could not find their way back to the hiking trail.

Use grammar clues to identify an unfamiliar word.

Name_____ Date_____

Reading Detective Practice #27

Directions: Fill in the blank with the adjective that best fits the sentence.
Check that the word you choose describes the right emotion.
Use letter-sound clues to help you.

(faithful　furious　bashful　baffled　panicky　pleased　calm　comical)

1. The b_____ boy would not say "Hello" to the other children.

2. José is the c_____ brother who is always telling jokes.

3. The campers were p_____ when they couldn't find their way out of the woods.

4. Jane's c_____ voice helped the worried children settle down.

5. The parents are p_____ with Daniel's excellent report card.

6. Brent has been a f_____ friend for more than 20 years.

7. Dad was f_____ when he saw black ink on the new carpet.

8. Mom was b_____ about where she left her gold bracelet.

Use grammar clues to identify an unfamiliar word.

Name_____ Date_____

Reading Detective Practice #28

Directions: Read the story below and fill in each blank with the adjective that makes sense.

All in an Afternoon

complete   hardworking   model   two   jumbo   satisfied   difficult

_____ **brothers** purchased a _____ **airplane kit**. When they

arrived home from the store, the boys ran quickly down to the basement to

assemble the plane. The model had so many parts that they decided to try it

step by step. First, they read the three pages of _____ **directions**.

Then, they made a _____ **list** of the parts and the steps to construct

the plane. Three hours later, these _____ **boys** had put together the

model of a _____ **airplane**. With _____ **looks** on their

faces, they raced upstairs to show the plane to their older sister. She checked

the model and told them they had done a great job.

Strategy 5

Strategy 5a. Identify nouns by locating noun determiners.
Strategy 5b. Identify verbs as action words that follow the subject noun.
Strategy 5c. Identify adjectives as words that describe nouns.

Use grammar clues to identify an unfamiliar word.

Name_____ Date_____

Reading Detective Practice #29

Directions: Write the correct part of speech (noun, verb, or adjective) for each underlined word.

1. Mrs. Rand placed a <u>generous</u> portion of potatoes on the plate. _____

2. The dog <u>made</u> those scratches on the door. _____

3. The <u>mall</u> opens early today. _____

4. Maya served the cookies on a <u>silver</u> tray. _____

5. The <u>bus</u> <u>departs</u> sharply at one o'clock. _____ _____

───────────── **On Your Own** ─────────────

Directions: Read the sentence and circle the part of speech that is missing.
Complete the sentence with a noun, verb, or adjective.
Check that the word you choose makes sense.

Missing Word

1. The rocket _____ off to space.   noun verb adjective

2. The _____ lights signaled for the traffic to stop.   noun verb adjective

3. Pairs of students _____ science experiments.   noun verb adjective

4. It took a long time to leave the _____ theater.   noun verb adjective

5. Mary gave us clear _____ to find her house.   noun verb adjective

Use grammar clues to identify an unfamiliar word.

Name_____ Date_____

Reading Detective Practice #30

Directions: Use the action verb in **bold** to find the adverb in each sentence. Write the adverb on the line.

> **Example:** Mom **lifted** the baby (gently) from the crib.
>
> **Answer:** *Gently* is the adverb in this sentence. The word *gently* tells *how* Mom lifted the baby.

Write the adverb that tells *how* the action happened.

1. The crowd **cheered** loudly during the show.   _____

2. Mother **tiptoed** softly into the baby's room.   _____

3. Jim and Joe quickly **ran** for shelter from the rain.   _____

Write the adverb that tells *when* the action happened.

4. Yesterday, we **played** at the park.   _____

5. Jackson **reads** nightly.   _____

6. Bill **painted** the fence today.   _____

Write the adverb that tells *where* the action happened.

7. The detective **looked** inside for the man.   _____

8. You may **sit** anywhere.   _____

9. The boys and girls **looked** everywhere for the puppy.   _____

Strategy 5

Use grammar clues to identify an unfamiliar word.

Name_____ Date_____

Reading Detective Practice #31

Directions: On the lines write *how, when,* or *where* to show what the underlined adverb is telling.

1. The package was delivered <u>early</u>.   _____

2. Ben <u>carefully</u> placed the glue on the paper.   _____

3. Tanya ran <u>upstairs</u> to get the model airplane.   _____

4. It is time to go <u>now</u>.   _____

5. The children sat <u>quietly</u> watching the movie.   _____

6. George looked <u>outside</u> for the dog.   _____

7. <u>Recently</u>, the family visited relatives in New York. _____

8. You followed her directions <u>correctly</u>.   _____

9. The family looked <u>everywhere</u> to find their lost dog. _____

Strategy 5

Use grammar clues to identify an unfamiliar word.

Name_____ Date_____

Reading Detective Practice #32

Directions: Complete each sentence with the correct adverb.
Check that the word you choose makes sense.

───────── **Part 1 — Adverbs That Tell *How*** ─────────

> **softly   suspiciously   sleepily   warmly   neatly   anxiously**

1. The children dressed _____ to play in the snow.

2. Mrs. Burns placed everything _____ into the drawers.

3. The boys watched _____ as the stranger walked up to the front door.

4. The kids walked _____ into the house after a full day at the amusement park.

5. The family waited _____ for Grandma and Grandpa to arrive.

6. Everyone walks _____ around the house when the baby is asleep.

───────── **Part 2 — Adverbs That Tell *When*** ─────────

> **afternoon   weekends   yesterday   monthly   immediately   early**

1. The neighbors called 911 _____ to report the accident.

2. They shop on _____ so there is enough food in the house during the week.

3. Lila does her homework every _____ when she gets home from school.

Use grammar clues to identify an unfamiliar word.

Name_____ Date_____

Reading Detective Practice #32 (continued)

4. Our teacher tells us to go to bed _____ to get a good night's rest for the next school day.

5. The Detective Club has only _____ meetings.

6. Maria is feeling much better because she took the medicine _____.

─────────────── **Part 3 — Adverbs That Tell *Where*** ───────────────

| under   downstairs   outside   inside   here   by   above |

1. Laura ran _____ to the basement for the tool kit.

2. Jason dropped his fork on the floor and looked for it _____ the table.

3. The boys and girls did not like staying _____ for three days during the blizzard.

4. Hamid called, "Look right _____! This is where we left the baseball glove."

5. Jack is too short to reach the cabinet _____ the kitchen sink.

6. _____ the wind is blowing leaves off the trees.

7. My cat loves to sit _____ my side and purr.

Strategy 5a. Identify nouns by locating noun determiners.
Strategy 5b. Identify verbs as action words that follow the subject noun.
Strategy 5c. Identify adjectives as words that describe nouns.
Strategy 5d. Identify adverbs as words that describe verbs.

Use grammar clues to identify an unfamiliar word.

Name_____ Date_____

Reading Detective Practice #33

―――――――――― **Part 1** ――――――――――

Directions: Circle *noun, verb, adjective,* or *adverb* to show what's missing.
Write a word in the blank that completes the sentence.
Check that the word you choose makes sense.

What's missing?

1. Latasha _____ home with
   her friends.   noun verb adjective adverb

2. "That was a _____ supper,"
   said Dad.   noun verb adjective adverb

3. Many new _____ arrived for
   the library.   noun verb adjective adverb

4. Chris looked _____ before he
   crossed the street.   noun verb adjective adverb

5. Monique had a _____ time at
   the party.   noun verb adjective adverb

6. The deer _____ into the woods. noun verb adjective adverb

7. This room needs _____ wallpaper. noun verb adjective adverb

8. _____ I went to the amusement park. noun verb adjective adverb

Strategy 5a. Identify nouns by locating noun determiners.
Strategy 5b. Identify verbs as action words that follow the subject noun.
Strategy 5c. Identify adjectives as words that describe nouns.
Strategy 5d. Identify adverbs as words that describe verbs.

Use grammar clues to identify an unfamiliar word.

Name_____ Date_____

Reading Detective Practice #33 (continued)

———————————— Part 2 ————————————

Directions: Use grammar clues to complete the story.
Fill in the blanks with nouns, verbs, adjectives, and adverbs that make sense.

One _____ Jerry and Jen _____ to the pet
           noun   verb

_____. They saw many _____ in the window. There
   noun   noun

was a _____ , _____ puppy in a box. Jerry and Jen
       adjective   adjective

went _____ to meet the puppy. They held him in their _____
     adverb (where)   noun

and fell in love with him. They _____ about the cost of the dog. Then,
                        verb

they _____ the shopkeeper they would come back_____
      verb   adverb (when)

with _____ parents to get the dog. The _____ day, Jen
     adjective   adjective

and Jerry _____ to the shop with their parents and _____
       verb   verb

the puppy. The children walked _____ out of the shop with their
                        adverb (how)

_____ friend.
   adjective

Tracks to Follow!

Grammar Clues

Readers use grammar clues to figure out unfamiliar words. These clues help us identify nouns, verbs, adjectives, and adverbs.

Strategy 5

a. **Identify nouns by locating noun determiners (*a, an, the,* and so forth)**

   Example: **The** children played in **the** house.

   Answer: *Children* and *house* are the nouns in this sentence. The determiner *the* comes before *children* and *house*.

b. **Identify verbs as action words that follow the subject noun. Verbs often take these forms: (1) root; (2) root + the ending *-s, -ing,* or *-ed*.**

   Example: The **children** ran to the ice cream truck.

   Answer: *Ran* is the verb in this sentence. *Ran* is the action word that follows the subject noun *children*.

c. **Identify adjectives as words that describe nouns. Adjectives tell *what kind, how many, whose,* or *which*.**

   Example: The happy **students** cheered for the team.

   Answer: *Happy* is the adjective in the sentence. *Happy* describes the noun *students*.

d. **Identify adverbs as words that describe verbs. Adverbs tell *how, when,* or *where*.**

   Example: Ben **ran** immediately to get help for the injured person.

   Answer: *Immediately* is the adverb in the sentence. It describes the verb *ran;* it tells how Ben ran.

Use the Clues! For the Teacher

Building on first-aid strategies 1 and 3 from Unit 1, the activities in this unit help students figure out unfamiliar words in context by referring to related words, phrases, and images. In this unit students will use the following strategies to figure out what unfamiliar words mean.

Strategy 6 Use key words in a passage to find a word's meaning.

a. Use keys words to find synonyms.
b. Use key words to find a synonym in the passage.
c. Use key words to check words with multiple meanings.
d. Use key words to find the meanings of unfamiliar phrases (idiomatic expressions).

Activities for Strategy 6:

❧ Use the context of a sentence or passage to find a synonym to substitute for a selected word.

❧ Find the correct synonym for a word with multiple meanings.

❧ Find the correct synonym or a similar phrase for an idiomatic expression.

Strategy 7 Use signal words to find synonyms and antonyms for an unfamiliar word.

a. Look for these words to signal synonyms: *or, is, is called, is known as, are, are called, are known as, was, was called, was known as, means, tells,* and *such as.*
b. Look for the word *but* to signal antonyms or opposite meanings.

Activity for Strategy 7:

❧ Use signal words (*or, but,* and so on) to find synonyms or antonyms for selected words.

Strategy 8 Use pictures to think of synonyms for an unfamiliar word.

Activity for Strategy 8:

❧ Use picture clues to find synonyms for selected words.

INTRODUCTORY MINI-LESSON

Present the sample sentences provided and ask students to come up with a substitute word that would make sense in each sentence. Record students' answers and then have them narrow the list by rereading the sentences with each of the substitute words to check for meaning. Discuss how using a synonym for an unknown word will help students continue reading without having to check the dictionary. Be sure to ask students to identify other clues in the surrounding language.

Sample sentences:

1. Bill **gloats** about his new bike. Have you seen him strutting around like a peacock?
2. The principal's comment, that she thinks our class is **competent**, tells me that we're a bunch of smart and able students.
3. The class **collaborated**, or worked together, to create a yearbook.
4. After the zoo animals escaped, there was **turmoil** in the city. People in cars swerved to avoid animals in the street, and many frightened pedestrians ran indoors and called for emergency help. The disruption was worsened by loud sirens.

STRATEGY AND PRACTICE PAGES

Distribute copies of page 52 to students. Read aloud and discuss meaning clues and the examples to be sure students understand how to use these strategies before they begin.

TIPS FOR TEACHING SEMANTIC-CUE STRATEGIES:

1. Use real-life reading materials—novels, newspapers, magazines, and passages from science and social studies textbooks to model the specific strategies in this unit.
2. Have students highlight or circle key words in the passages to show that they've found clues to word meanings.
3. Help build stronger student vocabulary by posting new words students have learned using semantic cues. Let students share their successes and newfound words during class meeting time, and have them create strategy charts on which they list the words and definitions. Refer to the chart regularly and use the new words in conversation to make them an integral part of students' vocabulary.

Use the Clues! For Students

Psst! Reading detectives search for **meaning cues** to solve the riddle of the unfamiliar word.

What are *meaning clues?*
These clues help you figure out a *synonym*, or substitute, for a word you don't know.

Strategy 6: Use key words in a passage to find a word's meaning.

a. Use key words to find synonyms.
> **Example:** The (robber) **conceals** the (money) bag on his bed inside a (pillow).

> **Answer:** *Conceals* means "hides." The robber *hides* money in his pillow so that no one can find it.

b. Use key words to find a synonym in the passage.
> **Example:** Bill **devoured** 48 hot dogs in ten minutes. He won first prize for (eating that much so quickly).

> **Answer:** *Devoured* means to "ate with great hunger." Bill ate 48 hot dogs in ten minutes.

c. Use key words to check words with multiple meanings.
> **Example:** Leslie won the tennis **match**.

> **Answer:** *Match* means "a contest." In this sentence *match* refers to a contest, not a stick you strike to light a fire.

d. Use key words to find the meanings of unfamiliar phrases (idiomatic expressions).
> **Example:** Malcolm is **sitting pretty** now that he has won the prize money.

> **Answer:** *Sitting pretty* means "to be in a great situation." Malcolm has the money to pay his bills and buy what he wants, so he's sitting pretty.

🔍 **Strategy 7:** Use signal words to find synonyms and antonyms (opposites) for an unfamiliar word.

    a. Look for these words to signal synonyms: *or, is, is called, is known as, are, are called, are known as, was, was called, was known as, means, tells,* and *such as.*

        Example: They decided not to buy the house because of the **labor**, or work, it would take to fix it.

        Answer: *Labor* means "work." *Or* signals that a synonym—*work*—is nearby.

    b. Look for the word *but* to signal antonyms or opposite meanings.

        Example: I am full of energy now, but I will be **exhausted** by the time I finish running the marathon.

        Answer: *Exhausted* means "very tired." *But* signals that a phrase with the opposite meaning—*full of energy*—is in the sentence.

🔍 **Strategy 8:** Use pictures to think of synonyms for an unfamiliar word.
        Example:

    A **prosperous** person lives in that house.

    Answer: *Prosperous* means *wealthy*. The size of the house tells us that the owner is wealthy.

Get Ready for Detective Work!
In this unit you will:
* use key words to select synonyms for words.
* use signal words to select meanings for words.
* use pictures to select meanings for words.

Strategy 6

Use key words in a passage to find a word's meaning.

Name_____ Date_____

Reading Detective Practice #34

Directions: Use the circled key words to help you choose two synonyms for the word in **bold**.
Underline your two choices, checking that the words make sense.

Example: The lost man **bellowed**, (Help me), help me! I'm (down in this hole)!"

   asked   shouted   ran   yelled

Answer: *Bellowed* means "shouted" or "yelled." A person lost and in danger would shout for help so that someone could hear him.

─────────────────── **Part 1** ───────────────────

1. The **brutal** (hurricane destroyed) the beach houses.

   curious   violent   satisfied   powerful

2. Jennifer, a **novice** skier, (must stay) on the slopes for people (just learning) to ski.

   beginning   new   adult   old

3. The **blissful** day for Mr. and Mrs. Adams was (March 1, 2001), the date of the (birth of their son).

   moody   joyful   torn   happy

4. "Having the (Super Bowl in this city) is a **major** (event for us)," (said the mayor).

   noisy   important   small   big

5. The (Red Cross) **furnishes** (food and clothing) to (flood victims).

   supplies   pulls   gives   builds

Strategy 6

Use key words in a passage to find a word's meaning.

Name_____ Date_____

Reading Detective Practice #34 (continued)

— Part 2 —

Directions: Underline all synonyms for the word in **bold**.
Circle key words in the sentence that help you choose the synonyms.
Check that the words you choose make sense.

1. Another parking garage provides **ample** parking spaces for the mall's shoppers.

   plenty   no   little   enough

2. Mother enjoys some **tranquil** time while the triplets are napping.

   noisy   quiet   screaming   peaceful

3. Mayor Dale was the **distinguished** speaker at the college graduation.

   respected   polite   kind   famous

4. **Weary** campers looked forward to resting at the end of the five-mile hike.

   sick   tired   worn-out   excited

Directions: Underline one synonym for the word in **bold** and circle key words.

5. Look at the **brilliant** diamonds in the queen's crown.

   messy   smart   sparkling

6. Jake **composed** a poem to give thanks to the volunteers.

   chose   drew   wrote

7. With rain and heavy fog, no one wanted to go out on that **dismal** evening.

   strange   cold   gloomy

Using Context Clues To Help Kids Tackle Unfamiliar Words   🐾 🐾 🐾 🐾 🐾 🐾 🐾 🐾 **55**

Use key words in a passage to find a word's meaning.

Name_____ Date_____

Reading Detective Practice #34 (continued)

8. When the lost hikers were found, they said, "We're **famished**. We haven't eaten in four days."

   hot   starving   cold

9. When travelers approached the bridge, they read the sign, "**Hazardous** driving on wet roads."

   snowy   dangerous   bumpy

10. Maria returned the **flawed** glass vase to the store. She explained to the clerk that there was a scratch on it.

    imperfect   beautiful   purple

11. "What kind of **dwelling** do you live in?" the museum guide asked us, as we passed through the igloo exhibit.

    house   workplace   garden

12. Billy **abhors** that awful-tasting medicine.

    likes   hates   whines

13. A **bevy** of young girls waited for the rap star to come out of the theater.

    van   group   cloud

14. Mr. Smith is **terminating** his business. He has decided to retire.

    starting   ending   beginning   joining

15. Mrs. Bender quickly drank a glass of water. "Ah," she said, "that soothes my **parched** throat."

    wet   oily   moist   dry

Use key words in a passage to find a word's meaning.

Name_____ Date_____

Reading Detective Practice #35

Directions: Read through the passage.
Underline the synonym for each word in **bold**.
Circle the key words that helped you.
Check that the word you choose makes sense.

Going Home from School

On an **ordinary** school day, Tom and Mike take the bus home from school.
normal, sunny

Today, after a **discussion**, the boys **concluded** they would walk home from
problem, talk   concentrated, decided

school. After all, it was a beautiful day. The boys were **engrossed** with baseball
tangled, busy

cards as they **strolled** down the street. They were **oblivious** to the turns they were
raced, walked   unaware, angry

making. When they did look around them, they were **bewildered**. The houses on
thoughtful, confused

the street did not look **familiar**. The boys were **baffled**! Where were they?
known, different   determined, confused

The boys approached a man painting the front of his house and told him

they were lost. This kind man **furnished** the boys with a map to guide them back
provided, checked

home. The map was **exceedingly** helpful. Twenty minutes later, the boys were
not really, very

elated to arrive home, but then they were embarrassed to give their mom an
saddened, happy

explanation for being so late. She had been **anxious** when the boys had not
reason, paper   delighted, worried

arrived home on time. Tom and Mike **confessed** that they had learned an
yelled, admitted

important lesson.

Strategy 6

Use key words in a passage to find a word's meaning.

Name_____ Date_____

Reading Detective Practice #36

Directions: Read through the passage.
Underline the synonym for each word in **bold**.
Circle the key words that helped you.
Check that the word you choose fits the sentence.

A New Home

One morning Maria sat on the front steps of her new apartment building

with a **forlorn** look on her face. Maria wished she could return to her **former**
sad, excited   old, new

neighborhood. She missed the many friends she had there. Maria's family had

just moved and she had not made any **acquaintances** yet. School did not start
friends, neighbors

for another month, and Maria was too **timid** to **roam** the neighborhood and
silly, shy   walk around, shout at

find some playmates. Her aunt saw Maria's **distress** and decided to help her.
happiness, suffering

Early that afternoon, Maria and her aunt **ambled** down the block together,
tore, walked

looking around and chatting. At the fifth door, they saw a mother braiding her

daughter's hair. Maria and her aunt stopped to say "Hello" and introduce

themselves to the neighbors. Maria and her aunt met Ms. Stoker and her

daughter, Samaya.

Samaya was excited to make a new friend. She invited Maria to go to the

park with her. All of a sudden, Maria had a **lighthearted** look on her face.
silly, happy

Today she had made friends with Samaya and no longer felt **isolated**.
crowded, alone

Strategy 6

Strategy 6a. Use key words to find a substitute word (synonym).

Use key words in a passage to find a word's meaning.

Name_____ Date_____

Reading Detective Practice #37

Directions: Circle the key words that help you understand the words in **bold**. Fill in the chart on page 60 with the meanings and key word clues.

1. The **jubilant** crowd cheered for the hometown football team.

2. "Wash those **grimy** hands before you sit down at the dinner table," said my older sister when we came in from digging an underground hideout.

3. The TV weatherman told the viewers to be prepared for changes! The temperatures would **fluctuate** for the next five days. He showed the following information:

Monday	Tuesday	Wednesday	Thursday	Friday
60°	50°	65°	55°	64°

4. Timothy **excelled** in swimming and had six trophies to show for it.

5. The grandparents were **ecstatic** with the birth of another grandchild.

6. Every Monday evening, laughter fills the room when the family watches that **hilarious** show.

7. The **keen** edge of this knife will cut through anything. Be careful when you use it!

8. **Masses** of people lined the streets to see the world-champion baseball team in the parade.

Use key words in a passage to find a word's meaning.

Name_____ Date_____

Reading Detective Practice #37 (continued)

Directions: Use this chart with page 59.

	Word	Meaning	Clues
1.	jubilant		
2.	grimy		
3.	fluctuate		
4.	excelled		
5.	ecstatic		
6.	hilarious		
7.	keen		
8.	masses		

Scholastic Teaching Resources

Use key words in a passage to find a word's meaning.

Name_____ Date_____

Reading Detective Practice #38

Directions: Read each passage.
Circle the synonym for the word in **bold** and write it on the line.

Example: City workers cleaned the **rubbish** from the corner lot. Many people dump (junk) on this lot.

Answer: *Rubbish* means junk. City workers would clear junk from a lot.
Junk is a synonym for *rubbish*.

---

1. Jamar was **astonished** to see friends and family when he opened the front door. Everyone sang "Happy Birthday." His surprised expression told them they had successfully kept the party a secret.

   Astonished means _____.

2. The principal announced over the intercom, "A **vehicle** is parked in front of the building. This car prevents the buses from getting through."

   Vehicle means _____.

3. Survivors of the fire paraded to the fire station with banners and balloons. They expressed their **gratitude** on the banners, which read, "Thanks to the people who saved our lives."

   Gratitude means _____.

4. Dad **saturates** the cloth with water. After it has been soaked, he pours spot remover on the stain.

   Saturates means _____.

5. A **penitent** kid told his parents, "I'm sorry I didn't tell you where I was going after school."

   Penitent means _____.

Use key words in a passage to find a word's meaning.

Name_____ Date_____

Reading Detective Practice #39

Directions: Read each passage.
Circle the synonym for the word in **bold** and write it on the line.

1. Grandma said, "What a **vivacious** host Simone is! This energetic young lady is serving food, entertaining guests, and having conversations with everyone."

   Vivacious means _____.

2. The boys were in **peril** as they sat on the rocks above the sea. They were in danger of being swept away by the strong waves.

   Peril means _____.

3. The speaker told such a **spellbinding** story that everyone moved forward in their seats, listening to every fascinating word that fell from her lips.

   Spellbinding means _____.

4. Mom said, "Make sure the gate is shut tight at the kitchen doorway. It needs to be **secure** so the puppy does not get into the living room."

   Secure means _____.

5. The **prime** meat served in this restaurant is the best you'll ever get.

   Prime means _____.

6. Sitting and staring out the window, Viviana **contemplated** what she should do. She was thinking about whether she should apologize to her sister or stay in her room a while longer.

   Contemplated means _____.

Strategy 6

Use key words in a passage to find a word's meaning.

Name_____ Date_____

Reading Detective Practice #40

Directions: Underline the correct meaning of the word in **bold**.
Use the circled key words as clues.

Example: The (soldiers) gathered **arms** to (protect) the fort.
    Arms is a word with multiple meanings.
        a. the limbs of the upper body, used for lifting and holding (*noun*)
        b. weapons (*noun*)

Answer: In this sentence *arms* means "weapons." The soldiers would use
        weapons for protection.

---

1. The (bank) has five other **branches** (in the city).

    a. limbs of a tree

    b. offices

2. Mr. Thomas told the workers that he would **dock** their pay because they were (late).

    a. place to tie up boats

    b. take away part of

3. You will be (charged) a **fine** if you are (caught throwing trash into the street).

    a. light, powdery

    b. amount of money owed for breaking the law

    c. good, okay

4. Every **float** (in the parade) was (made) of beautiful (flowers).

    a. moving decorated display

    b. stay on top of water

5. The **husky** was (pulling the sled) through the (snowy field).

    a. big and strong

    b. a type of dog

Use key words in a passage to find a word's meaning.

Name_____ Date_____

Reading Detective Practice #41

Directions: Underline the correct meaning for the word in **bold**. Use the circled key words as clues.

1. A swimmer began to **flounder** in the ocean and (yell for help).
   a. a kind of fish
   b. struggle

2. The (secretary) (takes) time to **file** (the papers).
   a. smooth something
   b. put away in an orderly fashion
   c. a folder of papers kept in a drawer

3. This (new company) wants to **court** the (best salesmen) to (work) for it.
   a. place to solve problems by the law
   b. place to play a game
   c. try to attract

4. There was a **grave** (situation) in the country after the earthquake.
   a. place for burying
   b. serious

5. Did the dog **dart** (into the street) to (get the ball)?
   a. dash, run quickly
   b. arrow thrown in a game
   c. sew a folded cloth to make a change in size

6. Captain Joe (writes) about his (sea adventures) in the **log**.
   a. a piece of wood
   b. a journal or diary

Use key words in a passage to find a word's meaning.

Name_____ Date_____

Reading Detective Practice #42

Directions: Fill in the blanks with the word in bold that completes each sentence. In the column on the right, write the number of the meaning that was used.

~~~~~~~~~~~~~~~~~ **Multiple Meaning Words** ~~~~~~~~~~~~~~~~~

prunes	1. cuts a bush or tree 2. fruit
racket	1. paddle in a tennis game 2. noise
root	1. cheer 2. underground part of plant
toll	1. fee, amount of money 2. to ring

Which meaning?

1. Ted does not like to eat _____. He thinks they're too mushy.   _____

2. Traffic is slow because everyone stops at the bridge to pay the _____.   _____

3. What was that _____ I heard in the middle of the night?   _____

4. The church bells _____ at the start of each hour.   _____

5. The gardener carefully _____ the bushes.   _____

6. The P.E. instructor showed the correct way to hold the _____.   _____

7. The dog pulled up the plant by the _____.   _____

8. The boys are going to _____ for the home team.   _____

(**Strategy 6**)

Strategy 6c. Use key words to check words with multiple meanings.

Use key words in a passage to find a word's meaning.

Name_____ Date_____

Reading Detective Practice #43

Directions: Fill in each blank with the word in **bold** that completes the sentence. In the column on the right, write the number of the meaning that was used.

~~~~~~~~~~~~~~~~~~~~~~~~~ **Multiple Meaning Words** ~~~~~~~~~~~~~~~~~~~~~~~~~

slip   1. fall   2. mistake, error   3. thin skirt worn under a dress

till   1. box or drawer for valuables   2. until   3. plow

toast   1. sliced, browned bread   2. a speech to honor someone

Which meaning?

1. Lila made a _____ , so now Benny knows about his surprise party.   _____

2. Each spring the farmer needs to _____ the soil.   _____

3. Our dad stood up to make a _____ to the bride and groom.   _____

4. The boys stole money from the _____ to buy a new game.   _____

5. The little girl's _____ was too long. It hung below the hem of her dress.   _____

6. Mother said, "Stand here _____ the bus arrives."   _____

7. Do you want jam on your _____ ?   _____

Use key words in a passage to find a word's meaning.

Name_____ Date_____

Reading Detective Practice #44

Directions: Use circled key words to help you understand the expression in **bold**. Underline the meaning of each expression.

Example: The girls were planning a (surprise party) for Jane. Brenda (warned), "Don't **let the cat out of the bag**, if you see Jane."

tell the secret   hide a cat   tie up a bag

Answer: *Let the cat out of the bag* means "tell the secret." If someone *lets the cat out of the bag*, Jane will not be surprised.

1. Mom is **tickled pink** that we (found shoes) to (match her dress).

   tickled pink: pink all over   happy   laughing from being tickled

2. Bill **turned red as a beet** when he was (caught snatching someone's book).

   turned red as a beet:

   moved something red   blushed with embarrassment   painted with red paint

3. This year Brittany **turned over a new leaf** and handed everything in on time.

   turned over a new leaf: made a change   raked leaves   pressed a leaf

4. The kids think that Jim will try to **weasel out of** the (challenge to eat fried worms).

   weasel out of: change   get out of doing   dig like a weasel

5. Bob **could not stomach** (watching the operation) on television and (walked out of the room).

   could not stomach:

   couldn't stand   had an operation   had a stomachache

Use key words in a passage to find a word's meaning.

Name_____ Date_____

Reading Detective Practice #45

Directions: Circle key words that help you understand the expression in **bold**. Underline the meaning of each expression.

1. "I'm **all ears**, and ready to learn about your three-week trip," said Rashid.

   all ears: pointed ears   ready to listen   playing an instrument

2. Jim made it to school **by the skin of his teeth** and was not marked late.

   by the skin of his teeth: brushing his teeth   brushing his skin   just in time

3. Do you know why Gina is so thin? She **eats like a bird**.

   eats like a bird: eats a small amount   flies to get food   eats worms

4. The two brothers were told to **quit horsing around** or someone would get hurt.

   quit horsing around:

   don't jump on a horse   stop playing so hard   stop walking so much

5. Sara and Kate like the same clothes, singers, school subjects, and just about everything else. They are **two peas in a pod**.

   two peas in a pod: like green peas   the same   sitting close together

6. Mr. Jones called in his workers to **pick their brains** on how to make more money.

   pick their brains:

   ask for ideas   give them toothpicks to use   put forks in their hair

Scholastic Teaching Resources

Strategy 7a. Look for these words to signal synonyms: *or, is, is called, is known as, are, are called, are known as, was, was called, was known as, means, tells,* and *such as.*

Use signal words to find synonyms and antonyms (opposites) for an unfamiliar word.

Name_____ Date_____

Reading Detective Practice #46

Directions: Write the synonym for the word in **bold**.
Use the signal word *or* to help you.

> **Example:** John **deletes**, *or* removes, files from the computer.
>
> **Answer:** *Deletes* means "removes." The word *or* tells us that a synonym for *deletes* is *removes.*

1. The **stout**, *or* plump, lady needs the next dress size up.

   Stout means _____ .

2. The detectives want to **interrogate**, *or* ask questions of, Mr. Fritz.

   Interrogate means _____ .

3. Shakira **perseveres**, *or* carries on, in an effort to read 100 books by the end of summer.

   Perseveres means _____ .

4. The class wrote letters to families of victims after the **catastrophe**, *or* disaster, of September 11, 2001.

   Catastrophe means _____ .

5. The police settled the **tumult**, *or* uproar, that took place at the hockey game.

   Tumult means _____ .

6. When the winds **diminish**, *or* lessen, the fishing boats can go out to sea again.

   Diminish means _____ .

Strategy 7

Strategy 7a. Look for these words to signal synonyms: *or, is, is called, is known as, are, are called, are known as, was, was called, was known as, means, tells,* and *such as.*

Use signal words to find synonyms and antonyms (opposites) for an unfamiliar word.

Name_____ Date_____

Reading Detective Practice #47

Directions: In each sentence, circle the signal word and underline the meaning of the word in **bold**.

Signal Words:

or, is, is called, is known as, are, are called, are known as, was, was called, was known as, were, were called, were known as, means, tells, such as

---

Example: A **simple grid system** ⓘs <u>the pattern of lines that help locate places on a map or globe</u>.

Answer: *Simple grid system* means "a pattern of lines that help locate places on a map or globe."
The meaning follows the signal word *is*.

～～～ Geography ～～～

1. Studying **landforms** means studying the different shapes of the Earth's surface.

2. A **plateau** is the landform that has steep sides and a flat top.

3. From the shore, we could see an **island**, or land surrounded on all sides by water.

4. Land that is surrounded by water on three sides is called a **peninsula**.

5. The low land that is between hills, mountains, and ranges is called a **valley**.

6. Very dry land with very few plants and little rainfall is known as a **desert**.

7. **Strait** means "a body of water that joins two larger bodies of water."

Strategy 7

Strategy 7a. Look for these words to signal synonyms: *or, is, is called, is known as, are, are called, are known as, was, was called, was known as, means, tells,* and *such as.*

Use signal words to find synonyms and antonyms (opposites) for an unfamiliar word.

Name_____ Date_____

Reading Detective Practice #47 (continued)

> **Signal Words:**
> *or, is, is called, is known as, are, are called, are known as, was, was called, was known as, were, were called, were known as, means, tells, such as*

~~~~~~~~~~~~ **Resources** ~~~~~~~~~~~~

1. **Resources** are things that can be used to produce a good or service.

2. A mall is a collection of stores that sell a variety of **goods**, such as toys, bikes, CD players, books, pizza, and many other things people want to buy.

3. **Natural resources** are things from nature that we use to provide goods and services. They include animals, plants, water, and wood.

4. **Capital resources** are goods and services made by people—for example, bridges, theaters, planes, and jewelry.

5. The goods and services that people want to have (clothing, cars, houses, and vacations, for example) are called **economic wants**.

6. The things we rely on every day, such as building houses, teaching school, and curing sickness, are known as **basic services**.

Strategy 7

Use signal words to find synonyms and antonyms (opposites) for an unfamiliar word.

Name_____ Date_____

Reading Detective Practice #48

Directions: Circle the meaning of the underlined word.
Use the signal word *but* to find an opposite meaning.
The words in **bold** will help you.

> **Example:** Usually Bob is **shy** about speaking in front of a large group, *but* he took a **bold** step and gave a speech to 500 people.
>
> happy   easy   (brave)
>
> **Answer:** *Bold* means "brave." When Bob, who is shy, gave a speech to 500 people, he was brave. *Bold* is the opposite of *shy* and means "brave."

1. The pirates **captured** the princess, *but* they said they would **release** her if she told them where to find the treasure.

    release: free   hold on to   keep forever

2. When I get **criticism** from my friends, I work harder; *but* when they **praise** my ideas, I feel happy.

    criticism: disapproval   statements   wisdom

3. Stretching makes your body **flexible**, *but* it can hurt if your body is **stiff**.

    flexible: bendable   hard   rocky

4. Beth's **optimistic** attitude helps her see the good in everything, *but* Sharon's **hopeless** attitude always makes her think things will never turn out right.

    optimistic: careless   cheerful   curious

5. Rushing through a test may cause you to make **mistakes**, *but* taking your time and checking the work helps you to be **accurate** on the test.

    accurate: writing   spelling   correct

Strategy 7

Use signal words to find synonyms and antonyms (opposites) for an unfamiliar word.

Name_____ Date_____

Reading Detective Practice #49

──────────────── **Part 1** ────────────────

Directions: In each sentence, circle the synonym for the underlined word. Use the signal word *or* to help you.

1. Mr. Upjohn made a **donation**, or gift, of $1,000 to help the school buy computers.

2. The **feeble**, or weak, man was not able to walk without the cane.

3. Frank wanted to visit the **remote**, or distant, island to get rest and relaxation.

4. The mayor **applauded**, or praised, the students for their math scores.

──────────────── **Part 2** ────────────────

Directions: Circle the meaning of the underlined word in each sentence. Use the signal word *but* to help you find the antonym and then circle it, too.

1. People cannot see through that **opaque** window, *but* they can see through the transparent one.

  What is the meaning of opaque?   (clear, foggy)

  What is the meaning of transparent? (clear, foggy)

2. It would be **ridiculous** to stay up all night, *but* sensible to get a good night's rest and be fresh in the morning.

  What is the meaning of ridiculous? (wise, silly)

  What is the meaning of sensible? (wise, silly)

Strategy 8

Use pictures to think of synonyms for an unfamiliar word.

Name_____ Date_____

Reading Detective Practice #50

Directions: Circle the meaning of the word in **bold**. Use the picture to help you
find a synonym.

Example: The first-place runner's face was **radiating** happiness.

Answer: *Radiating* means *"shining"* or *"glowing."* The runner is so happy that
her face is *shining* or *glowing* with happiness.

1. The truck will **transport** the family's belongings to the new house.

   transport:　　　　　sell　　　　　　　　move　　　　　build

2. Mary's house is located on a busy **thoroughfare**.

   thoroughfare:　　　street　　　　　　　hill　　　　　traffic

3. The shy girl was **reluctant** to enter her new classroom.

   reluctant:　　　　unwilling　　　　　　happy　　　　joyful

❖❖ ❖❖ ❖❖ ❖❖ ❖❖ ❖❖ ❖❖ ❖❖ Using Context Clues To Help Kids Tackle Unfamiliar Words

Name_____ Date_____

Reading Detective Practice #51

Directions: Circle the meaning of the word in **bold**. Use the picture to help you find a synonym.

1. Mr. Rodriguez showed his friend a picture of the old desk that he **salvaged** from the garbage dump.

   salvaged: sold   destroyed   rescued

2. Bill had **oodles** of boxes to give to Tom.

   oodles: many   few   little

3. Jackson **sprinted** down the street to get home in time for dinner.

   sprinted: hopped   ran   walked

4. Thomas **peers** through the microscope.

   peers: touches   looks   pokes

Strategy 8

Use pictures to think of synonyms for an unfamiliar word.

Name_____ Date_____

Reading Detective Practice #52

Directions: Circle the meaning of the word in **bold**. Use the picture to help you find a synonym.

1. After school, this **duo** went to a baseball game.

   duo:　　　　　　piece　　　　　　pair　　　　　　part

___

2. As the kids walked, they saw Mr. Tibble **repairing** the lawn mower.

   repairing:　　　　fixing　　　　　　trying　　　　fighting with

___

3. Farther down the street, Mr. Bill was **toiling** on the engine of his car.

   toiling:　　　　rushing　　　　　working　　　　playing

___

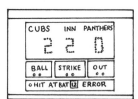

4. The kids were late arriving at the park, and the game had **commenced** without them.

   commenced:　　　played　　　　　started　　　　jumped

❀❀ ❀❀ ❀❀ ❀❀ ❀❀ ❀❀ ❀❀ ❀❀ Using Context Clues To Help Kids Tackle Unfamiliar Words

Tracks to Follow!

Meaning Clues

**Readers use meaning clues to find
substitutes for the words they don't know.**

Strategy 6

a. Use keys words to find synonyms.

Example: The **blustery** (wind bit at our skin) and (howled) in
our ears.

Answer: *Blustery* mean "violently blowing." Wind that bites
at skin and howls is *blustery*.

b. Use key words to find a synonym in the passage.

Example: Looking at the **overcast** sky, Dad told us it was
too (cloudy) to go to the beach.

Answer: *Overcast* means "cloudy." The cloudy, or *overcast*,
sky meant that it was not a beach day.

c. Use key words to check words with multiple meanings.

Example: The directions say to take a right at the **fork** in
the road.

Answer: In this sentence, *fork* is a place where the road
separates, going in two different directions. *Fork*
does not mean here "an eating utensil."

**d. Use key words to find the meanings of unfamiliar phrases
(idiomatic expressions).**

Example: Jay was **walking on eggshells** around his angry
older brother.

Answer: The expression *walking on eggshells* means "careful
not to bother or annoy." Jay was careful not to
annoy his angry older brother, so we say he was
walking on eggshells.

Tracks to Follow!

Meaning Clues

**Readers use meaning clues to find
substitutes for the words they don't know.**

Strategy 7

a. **Look for key words to signal a synonym. (Synonym signal words include *or, is, is called, is known as, are, are called, are known as, was, was called, was known as, means, tells,* and *such as.*)**

Example: The police officer **apprehended**, *or* arrested, the burglar.

Answer: *Apprehended* means "arrested." *Or* signals that a word with a similar meaning—*arrested*—is nearby.

b. **Look for the word *but* to signal antonyms or opposite meanings.**

Example: The babysitter was **lax** about the rules at first, *but* had to be strict when the kids started fighting.

Answer: *Lax* means relaxed. *But* signals that a word with an opposite meaning—*strict*—is nearby.

Strategy 8

Use pictures to think of synonyms for an unfamiliar word.

Example:

The grass in the baseball diamond was perfectly **manicured**.

Answer: *Manicured* means "trimmed neatly." The even, neat shape of the field shows that the grass is trimmed neatly.

Unit 1: First-Aid Strategies

page 8, #1
1. lightning
2. ambulance
3. hammer
4. cold
5. worried
6. shovels

page 9, #2
1. popcorn
2. apples
3. ice cream
4. hot dog
5. turkey
6. spaghetti
7. ice cube
8. tomato

page 10, #3
Acceptable answers:
1. jelly, jam
2. sugar, sweetener
3. cob
4. pancakes, waffles
5. sundaes, syrup
6. cereal
7. beans
8. cake

page 11, #4
On the Farm
1. tractor
   (rides around, clear the land, dig rows)
2. house
   (leaves, returns be with his family, warm, comfortable)
3. cows
   (provide the farmer's family and others, healthy drink)
4. hay
   (in the horse's stall)
5. horses
   (in the barn, farmer gives it a piece of sugar)
6. barn
   (big red, stores tools, keep horses there, protect them from cold and rain)

Can You Name the Animals on Your Own?
1. rooster
2. pigs
3. sheep
4. turkey

page 12, #5
1. hitter, fielder, coach, strike, umpire
2. flowers, hose, shovel, vegetables
3. obeys, barks, bowl, bone,
4. strange, old, scary, bats, creaks
5. diving, shallow, goggles, flippers
6. bunk, hikes, counselors, activities

page 13, #6
1. purr, whiskers, tabby, fur
2. tiger, trapeze, ringmaster, clowns, elephants
3. sidewalks, crowd, taxi-cabs, skyscraper, traffic
4. detective, searching, clues, mystery, thief
5. explore, dark, hidden, dangerous
6. mountains, rivers, oceans, lakes, islands

page 14, #7
Circled words: cake, games, balloons, presents, friends
1. friends
2. cake
3. presents
4. games
5. balloons
Other acceptable words: party favors, food, music, playing

pages 15–16, #8
Students must accurately decode these words:
1. register
2. coupon
3. receipt
4. escalator
5. jewelry
6. elevator
7. perfume
8. bundles

page 17, #9
1. patients
2. nurse
3. stethoscope
4. prescription

page 18, #10
1. throne
2. servant
3. crown
4. balcony
5. princess

Unit 2: Graphophonic Cues

page 22, #11
Students must accurately decode these words:
1. recognize
2. expensive
3. celebrate
4. imaginations
5. situation
6. medication
7. thirsty
8. canceled
9. demonstrates, chemicals

page 23, #12
1. parade
2. exercise
3. substitute
4. garage
5. little
6. smell
7. rake
8. toothbrush
9. score

page 24, #13
1. mountain
2. blood
3. treasure
4. horseback
5. honest
6. furniture
7. forecast
8. caution

page 25, #14
1. bandage
2. correct
3. correct
4. helicopter
5. full
6. fastest
7. watch
8. fly
9. correct

page 26, #15
1. sudden
2. heard
3. accident
4. intersection
5. offered
6. grateful
7. concern
8. praised

Unit 3: Syntactic Cues

page 30, #16
1. horse, town
2. kids, boat, lake
3. machine, coins
4. principal, microphone
5. troll, bridge
6. alligator, swamp
7. Uncle
8. ocean
9. kitchen
10. dictionary

page 31, #17
1. stars
2. correct
3. bus
4. ladder
5. mechanic
6. pilot
7. balloons
8. bench
9. correct

page 32, #18
Circled words: camera, beach, sunscreen, clothes, diary, photographs, goggles
1. clothes
2. beach
3. goggles
4. diary
5. seashells
6. sunscreen
7 camera
8. photographs

page 33, #19
1. astronaut
2. police officer
3. lawyer
4. teacher
5. musician
6. doctor

page 34, #20
1. protected
2. held
3. skate
4. is reading
5. stretches
6. chops
7. starts
8. rushes
9. drinks

page 35, #21
1. rescued
2. correct
3. correct
4. looked
5. correct
6. correct
7. jogged
8. threw

page 36, #22
Part 1
1. gathered
2. announced
3. raise
4. liked
5. talked
6. agreed

Part 2
1. came
2. pointed
3. examined
4. sold
5. contributed

page 37, #23
1. mumbled
2. groaned
3. cautioned
4. announced
5. sobbed
6. advised

page 38, #24
Acceptable answers:
1. play, jump, run, walk—verb
2. people, workers—noun
3. scared, frightened—verb
4. rocket—noun
5. magician—noun
6. built, made, constructed—verb
7. ran, scurried—verb
8. ate, orders, eats—verb
9. cheese, sausage, onion—noun

page 39, #25
1. soft, furry
2. old, broken-down
3. shiny
4. sticky
5. stuffy
6. strange, shadowy
7. salty, spicy, sour, juicy
8. dirty, squeaky, noisy, speedy, shiny
9. plastic, striped, enormous,

blue
page 40, #26
1. suspicious
2. smiling
3. curious
4. shallow
5. modern
6. rude
7. rotten
8. confused

page 41, #27
1. bashful
2. comical
3. panicky
4. calm
5. pleased
6. faithful
7. furious
8. baffled

page 42, #28
1. two
2. model
3. difficult
4. complete
5. hardworking
6. jumbo
7. satisfied

page 43, #29
1. adjective
2. verb
3. noun
4. adjective
5. noun, verb

On Your Own
Acceptable answers:
1. soared, flew, shot—verb
2. red, flashing—adjective
3. worked on, completed—verb
4. crowded, packed—adjective
5. directions—noun

page 44, #30
1. loudly
2. softly
3. quickly
4. yesterday
5. nightly
6. today
7. inside
8. anywhere
9. everywhere

page 45, #31
1. when
2. how
3. where
4. when
5. how
6. where
7. when
8. how
9. where

pages 46–47, #32
Part 1
1. warmly
2. neatly
3. suspiciously
4. sleepily
5. anxiously
6. softly

Part 2
1. immediately
2. weekends
3. afternoon
4. early
5. monthly
6. yesterday

Part 3
1. downstairs
2. under
3. inside
4. here
5. above
6. outside
7. by

pages 48–49, #33
Part 1
Acceptable answers:
1. walks, runs, rides—verb
2. good, delicious, wonderful, awful—adjective
3. books, tapes, cassettes—noun
4. carefully, quickly, all around—adverb
5. grand, wonderful, bad—adjective
6. ran, darted, jumped—verb
7. colorful, new, striped, floral—adjective
8. today, yesterday, last month—adverb

Part 2
Acceptable answers:
1. day, morning
2. walked, ran
3. store, shop
4. animals, pets, birds, dogs, kittens, puppies
5. cute, playful, little
6. (same answers as 5)
7. inside
8. arms
9. asked
10. told
11. today, in the afternoon, tomorrow, later
12. their, both
13. same, next
14. went, returned
15. bought, purchased
16. happily, joyfully
17. cute, adorable, little, new

Unit 4: Semantic Cues
pages 54–56, #34
Part 1
1. violent, powerful
2. beginning, new
3. joyful, happy
4. important, main
5. supplies, gives

Part 2
1. plenty, enough
2. quiet, peaceful
3. respected, famous
4. tired, worn-out
5. sparkling
6. wrote
7. gloomy
8. starving
9. dangerous
10. imperfect
11. house
12. hates
13. group
14. ending
15. dry